Which Islam? Whose Islam? and other essays

Which Islam? Whose Islam? and other essays

Zuhdi Jasser

Connor Court Publishing

Published in 2019 by Connor Court Publishing

Copyright © Zuhdi Jasser as a collection, chapter 6: Steve Postal

All rights reserved. No part of this book may be reproduced or transmitted in any form or by any means, electronic or mechanical, including photocopying, recording or by any information storage and retrieval system, without prior permission in writing from the publisher.

Connor Court Publishing Pty Ltd.
PO Box 7257
Redland Bay QLD 4165
sales@connorcourt.com
www.connorcourt.com

Phone 0497 900 685

ISBN: 978-1-925826-36-4

Cover design Maria Giordano

Printed in Australia

Contents

1 Which Islam? Whose Islam? Part 1 of 4   9

2 Which Islam? Whose Islam? Part 2 of 4   21

3 Which Islam? Whose Islam? Part 3 of 4   25

4 Which Islam? Whose Islam? Part 4 of 4   31

5 Understanding the Cauldron that Brewed ISIS   41

6 A Muslim Reformer Explains How to Fight Islamism   53

7 Why A "Ritual Nick" Is a Smoke Screen for Female Genital Mutilation   73

8 Fighting for Victory against Islamism   75

9 Can a Western Islam Emerge?   83

10 An Epilogue From my book: *A Battle for the Soul of Islam: An American Patriot's Fight to Save his Faith*   99

Preface

This collection of articles offer a snapshot of Muslim Reformist Dr Zuhdi Jasser preceding his March 2019 Islam + Islamism Tour in Australia. Jasser claims we need a 'jihad against jihad' to defend western secular democracy. Some will cry 'alarmist' and hotly contest the need for an American born Muslim to wage an ideological war within the House of Islam. But let's face it; there are some alarming activities within the House, even in Australia.

At the Sydney 2007 Hizb ut- Tahrir conference I purchased a book called *Democracy is a System of Kufr* (infidel). This instructed Australian Muslims that it was forbidden to adopt, implement or call for democracy and in support of this, one lecture offered a three-point plan on how to overturn democracy and impose the Islamic State. The ideological struggle to alter public opinion was point 2 in this grand plan. It is this pre-cursor to violent Islamism, the non-violent ideological war, which Jasser maintains we must address head on as the root cause of terrorism. Non-violent dawah, the ideological mission and violent jihad, are two sides to the same coin. Whatever way that coin falls its heads up for global Islamists.

These pages challenge governments and ordinary

citizens to stand on the side of all liberty minded people, Muslim and non-Muslim, and offer hope for a healthier free and democratic future for all.

-- Vickie Janson

1

Which Islam? Whose Islam? Part 1 of 4

All Muslims Own the Interpretation of the Koran

August 24, 2007

The world is just beginning to finally peel the onion of political Islam (Islamism). The central question is what lies at the core? Devotional anti-Islamist Muslims generally believe that at the core of Islamism, is neither a religion nor a faith. It is a global political movement and ideology falsely cloaked in a religion of the God of Abraham. How does a reform-minded Muslim go about proving such a supposition? Do we even need to? Whose interpretation of the Koran is more valid? Do we believe the peaceful Muslim interpretation or the Wahhabi-Jihadist one? More importantly, as we seek the preservation of our homeland security against radical Islamists, we finally realize a growing need for pious Muslims to articulate a clear alternative narrative to the intolerant anti-liberty Islamist political construct.

Only dedicated Muslims can answer these questions with credibility. Most Muslims just want to live and enjoy their daily lives, raise their children, go to work, and contribute to their local communities. The faith they actually practice in the belly of the liberty and freedom of America is most often quite reformed and liberalized in the daily constructs of their acceptance and internalization of pluralism. This has been generally by virtue of assimilation into the culture of Western enlightenment to which they have accommodated their own personal theological underpinnings. While a faith without a clergy lends itself to this accommodation of personal theological ideas, the established academic theology of Islamic jurisprudence is far behind and in desperate need of a renewed ijtihad (modern interpretation).

The Islamist leadership of the Islamic community, however, has generally not reflected the ideas of many, if not most, Western Muslims and has remained driven and radicalized by an overriding religious legal construct (Shari'a) still dated in the 15th century and also driven by 19th century Wahhabi fundamentalist radicalism and 20th century political Islam. The counter movements to any of this have been stifled by many factors. However, most suffocating have been the despots, dictators, and ruthless monarchs of the Muslim world which killed individual inquiry and created a corruption brought to the West with many Muslim immigrants. The three-headed global snake of secular dictatorships, political Islam, and oil-funded Wahhabism in the 20th century has quashed any real opportunities for a second Muslim enlightenment – one that brings in a post-modern era. For those Muslims living in freedom in the West, our counter movements have been stifled by apathy, ignorance, moral weakness, and control of most major Islamic organizations by Islamists. To this, these organizations would respond with denial. But I challenge them to produce any anti-Wahhabi, anti-Islamist texts, interpretations, or sermons of any impact or persistence from their Islamist teachers and enablers. From the Islamic Society of North America (ISNA) to the Assembly of Muslim Jurists of America, they have remained driven and often funded by Wahhabi and Islamist interests who live and breathe political Islam.

There is no getting past the fact that every people and nation ultimately get the "government they deserve" by virtue of their own action or inaction. It is the same principle for our religious leadership, academia, mosques, and activist organizations within the Muslim community. As Muslims, unless we intellectually take on the fundamentalists, the Wahhabis, the Jihadis, and the Islamists for the intellectual reigns of our faith, we ultimately abrogate our ideology to their imams, clerics, and so-called *ulemaa* (scholars). The fact that I have a difficult time finding non-Islamist (or better yet, anti-Islamist Muslim) theological texts with which to teach my children is a serious problem to which few Muslims will own up.

The anti-Islamist Muslim narrative will only be credible if it includes a counter-Jihad which provides alternative Koranic interpretations to passages exploited by militant Islamists to divide their world into "Muslim and non-Muslim" or "Islam and War." The answer from anti-Islamist Muslims must be founded in Koranic interpretations which comfortably articulate an Islam that can theologically defend Western secular democracies based upon universal principles of liberty.

This debate is usually roundly ignored by the mainstream media, which unfairly allows American Islamist organizations like CAIR (Council on American Islamic Relations), MPAC (Muslim Public Affairs Council), ISNA (Islamic Society of North America), ICNA (Islamic Circle of North America) and the MAS (Muslim American Society) to speak for all American Muslims. Their Islamist response to the release of last week's NYPD Terror Report on "Radicalization in the West: the Homegrown Threat" is a classic example of the unwillingness of the likes of CAIR and MPAC to publicly counter the radical ideologies of political Islam, which are the root cause of terrorism.

The NYPD Report begins the long overdue discussion of beginning to understand the theological transformation of an individual (a militant Islamist) from peace-loving nationalist to global Jihadist.

To counter the Jihadist interpretation, we must disseminate peaceful interpretations of the same Koranic text especially in what appear to be the more troublesome passages utilized by Jihadists.

I am not formally an expert in Koranic Arabic or *Shari'a* (Islamic law). But when the academic institutions of Islamic theology have been corrupted, this may in fact be somewhat of an asset as long as one uses interpretations that can be legitimately derived from the Arabic text of the Koran based upon reason. Born in the U.S. and raised in Wisconsin, my formal education is in medicine and biomedical ethics with military medical training. But unlike the practice of medicine, I was raised by my devout Muslim parents, believing that the practice of my faith of Islam required neither a license nor a degree and was accountable only to God. A lifetime of Koranic and Islamic recitation, education, prayer, and practice are foundation enough for the right to hold valid opinions regarding the Koran and its interpretation. While this interpretation may be at odds with many of the so-called clerics and *ulemaa* of today, this should not shake the common Muslims' ability to interpret our own faith in our personal relationship with God. In a free market of ideas, it is our duty to provide a liberty narrative and interpretation of Islam which counters the Islamists.

The Koran tells me that there is no clergy, no intermediaries, in our faith. All it takes to be a Muslim is to believe (bear witness) in the God of Abraham and the Message of the Prophet Mohammed. No other Muslim can tell me I'm not a Muslim and similarly, I cannot do the same. I can speak about Islamic behavior, ideologies, and practice, but *takfir* (apostasy: to deny a Muslim his chosen faith) is something only God can do on the Day of Judgment after our passing according to the Islam I was taught – no matter what the Wahhabis and Islamists may say. Apostasy laws are a prime example of what happens when Islamists have control of society's legal venues. Similarly, blasphemy laws argue that the domain of religious scholars should be protected from critique. Post-modern society allows freedom of religion but not freedom from criticism or freedom from being offended. Islamists would use blasphemy laws to prevent valid critique of the political Islamist state. There are in fact, Islamic refutations to the imposition of blasphemy laws based upon universal religious freedom for all which can be argued within a liberty minded Islam.

There is no "communication" or "excommunication" for that matter involved in my being a Muslim. It is a complete free-for-all, with no institution providing or guaranteeing membership other than God. My faith, as I was taught, comes to me by virtue of my own choice and personal relationship with God. The Koran, to me as a Muslim, is God's message. But the inspiration for my soul comes from within and is strengthened by my inner relationship with God. The text, God's scripture, only validates that relationship. It is presented in the Koran as it was revealed in a setting, a history, of the 7th century, which Muslims need to separate from the religion which lives on today. Religion must modernize through *ijtihad* (re-interpretation) in order to stay relevant and relegate the outdated experiences to history. Without re-interpretation and separation of history from religion, it freezes in time and conflicts with modernity. The root cause of terrorism today is this conflict vis-à-vis political Islam and its conflict with Western secular democracy.

The tenor of the interpretation of the Islamic scripture is driven by the moral principles which I carry to the text. I believe that most simply look within God's text for affirmation or denial of previously made conclusions, universal principles, concerning their own established moral precepts in life. It is not the text itself which teaches or creates the love or hate to which so many incorrectly ascribe it. It is the teachers, mentors, and parents who provide an interpretation of the Arabic Koran who ultimately become the disseminators and creators of the ideology, rather than God. The Arabic text is a fixed communication from God, in the Arabic language at the time of Mohammed, in the belief of Muslims. It is up to Muslims to interpret it and re-interpret it in other languages and in context to fit yesterday and today.

Similarly, the debates within the faith of Islam as to the interpretation of what is and what is not *Islamic* behavior and theology should be open to every Muslim with equal access. The discourse should always be founded in reason. Once reason gives way to the clerical attempt to control us by exerting a monopoly of understanding of God's intention, Islamism will surge to further domination.

One of the greatest steps forward we can make as a faith community is to believe that *ijtihad* (modern interpretation) is not only open to every Muslim, but also our obligation as practitioners of our faith. The first great step toward reformation within Islam against political Islam will only come when we deconstruct the intellectual elitism of the *ulemaa* (Islamic scholars). Often, even some of the most reform-minded *ulemaa* who are formally trained in Islamic jurisprudence and theology and thus carry a sense of entitlement, have a very difficult time accepting the criticism and opinions of pious Muslims who have not been granted entry into the "brotherhood" of clerics and scholars of Islam.

This is the age-old theocratic mechanism of stifling debate and maintaining control of a religious community by the clerics and *imams* (religious teachers). They first declare the non-scholar (non- professorial) interpretations of our own religious texts to be invalid because their source is not learned. They then state that there can be no more debate since the "non-imam" Muslim has been discredited. The determination of who is and who is not learned is only the domain of the *ulemaa* (scholars). As far as the imams are concerned, the practice and study of a faith for one's entire life, or years for that matter, does not suffice to provide a basis for holding strong convictions regarding scriptural and legal interpretations. Ultimately, this is the difference between theocracy and societies based upon liberty. Liberal societies focus upon ideas and reason, while theocracies focus upon the mandate and power of the theocrats who believe they are the representatives of God and only their interpretation of His text is valid.

Thus, real Muslim reform needs two elements. Not only do we need to "open the doors of *ijtihad*" (re-interpretation) again, but open the rules of engagement to encourage and respect a very public discourse which equally values the input of every single Muslim regardless of "training."

Thus, one of the foundational principles of our American Islamic Forum for Democracy was that we affirm the "inalienable right of *every* Muslim to be *equally* entitled to their opinion concerning their own interpretation of the religion of Islam and its scriptures. We refuse to accept subservience of the interpretation of our personal faith and personal relationship with God to *imams* (teachers and prayer leaders) and other *ulemaa*." While certainly religious teachers are central to those seeking knowledge and learning, the choice of teacher and sources (which can be infinite) is up to the individual and not the community. Once the teacher becomes community leader and politician he is no longer a spiritual teacher but rather a theocrat. Accountability of faith ultimately resides with God and no one else.

Some would argue that this defies respect for the academia of theology. This could not be further from the truth. One can believe in the virtue of reason and the equal access to it by all while also condemning theocracy, theocrats, and their creeping controls over the community. At the end of the day, the prevailing interpretations of Islam in 2007 are those which are offered by the Muslims of today and by those Muslims who choose and who have the moral courage to engage in the debate.

The only way in which we can defeat Wahhabism and its associated global Jihadism and Islamism is to open the access of interpretation of our scripture to all Muslims who love the faith and choose to practice it. The Islamists will ultimately fall defeated in discredit and disgrace by the reasoning of enlightened liberty-minded anti-Islamist Muslims of the West when we finally wake up to their religious legitimacy simply as practicing Muslims. We should look back at previous religious reformation in Christianity, for example, and the separation of church and state which created America. While obvious differences with Islam exist, centrally, the premise of change against theocracy is the same. The faith of Islam and its current pseudo-clergy in control can only be modernized and displaced from the bottom up. Theocrats, like any autocrat and despot, seek to maintain control at all costs – regardless of reason and universal humanitarian principles.

This discussion sets the stage for a long overdue public debate within the Muslim community about passages in the Koran which are currently being bandied about the Internet. How do "good Muslims" differ from radical ones insofar as the practice of religion and its interpretation from their same Koran? How do we reconcile some of the difficult more violent passages of the Koran with life today? And under what authority?

I will begin to try and address some of these issues from my own personal perspective in my next column. It was, however, first important to discuss the legitimacy with which a non-cleric, *non- ulemaa* like myself and so many other like-minded anti-Islamist Muslims can and should express a post-modern interpretation of Islamic scripture in the Koran. A palpable movement of Muslims can begin to create an expression of a post-modern interpretation of our Arabic Koran. This interpretation can be at home with American liberty and freedom.

The so-called scholars of the now politically defunct Christian clerics of the Church of England of the 18th century suffered a similar fate. Hopefully this struggle for Muslims won't be as bloody, but the signs are it may. Anti-Islamist Muslims will defeat political Islam when they find and articulate universal liberty and freedom from our own scripture while preserving our own spiritual Islam. This will require a bottom-up re-interpretation of the Koran which is much needed in this tumultuous point in history. This is most likely the only way for us to see the root cause of terrorism finally disappear.

2

Which Islam? Whose Islam?
Part 2 of 4

All Muslims Own the Interpretation of the Koran
September 12, 2007

As we note the sixth anniversary of the horrific attacks of 9/11, we in the Muslim community need to begin a serious intellectual deconstruction of "bin Ladenism," its origins, and all of its offshoots and ideological siblings – which form the nucleus of the phenomenon of political Islam (Islamic supremacism, or Islamism) and Jihadism.

Americans are now reviewing the recent video message from bin Laden, whose delivery was timed to preface our annual mourning of the victims of his cowardly attack. Despite the denials of many "leading" Muslim organizations in America, bin Laden's mantra is not that of an isolated psychopath. Rather, as Daveed Gartenstein-Ross writes, it is the rant of an imperialist a manifesto of militant Islamism, which deserves the full resources of the American Muslim community to defeat.

Bin Laden's mantra is derived from Wahabi teachings (extremism founded in late 19th century Saudi Arabia), and its associated Jihadism and caliphism (the desire to build an oppressive Islamist empire, or "caliphate"). Throughout the world, we are witnessing the growth of various militant Islamist organizations that share, as their common motivating mission, the drive to create intercontinental Islamic states, at all costs. Their militantly Jihadist interpretation of the Koran serves as both the root cause and moral justification for their vision, and the actions they take to realize it.

If Muslims wish to defeat the fervent believers of Jihadism and Islamism, we must begin by deconstructing and defeating their claim to moral sanction – and even divine commandment – to perpetrate their acts of intolerance, murder and oppression. The time has come (indeed, it is long overdue) for anti-Islamist Muslims to begin offering alternative interpretations of the Koran to political and militant Islamists who, unfortunately, are the focus of the lion's share of everything the world currently sees, hears, and reads about Islam.

It is time to argue ideas, and not 'qualifications'

In my first column of this series, last column (Part I) I set the stage for the beginning of just such a discussion. I reassert the fact that I am not a formal expert in Koranic

Arabic, or in sharia (Islamic jurisprudence).

I am, however, schooled in enough disciplines to understand the general principles of intellectual derivations, and the underpinnings of language, meaning, interpretation, history, religion, and faith. My interpretations are made through the lens of a devout anti-Islamist Muslim, as well as an advocate for universal liberty. A plurality of Muslims – if not a majority – are non-Islamist or better yet, *anti*-Islamist, and have pragmatically reconciled our faith with the principles of universal religious freedom. But the vast majority of us have had neither the mentorship nor the courage to take on the so-called *ulamaa's* (Islamic scholars') interpretations of the Koran. Similarly, we have allowed many articulate, diligent non-Muslim critics of Jihadism and Islamism to rely solely on Jihadist/ Wahabiist interpretations of Islam, and have not provided them with reasoned, academic refutations and alternative interpretations.

Sadly, the result is that most "mainstream" Muslim organizations rely upon claims of victimization and "Islamophobia" to deflect both internal and external criticism of Jihadism and Islamism – claims that are manifestly illegitimate, and serve only to undermine our faith.

While a truly legitimate refutation of the myopic, exclusively Jihadist/Islamist interpretation of Koran would take a full textbook, even a taste of such a discussion will provide an example of how a Muslim can read his or her Koran free of Islamism. This is the real work we need to do – and this is what *must* be done if we are to undermine those who seek to cultivate yet another generation of Jihadists and Islamists.

There can be no room for denial or equivocation in this reinterpretation. But I am confident that we can have a candid and forthright assessment of the divergent views of Islam. If along with this there is also a willingness to separate history from religious doctrine, and couch it in the underlying principles of the nation-states founded in freedom – we can win the war of ideas against monsters like bin Laden, and all his ideological brethren.

In part three, I will discuss interpretation of the Koran, both by laymen and through the lens of freedom.

3
Which Islam? Whose Islam? Part 3 of 4

All Muslims Own the Interpretation of the Koran
September 13, 2007

Whose interpretation of the Koran is Islam?

While most English translations of the Koran are similar, there are essential differences that may escape non-Muslims, including its well-intentioned and articulate critics. Actually, these differences are better termed *human interpretations* rather than *translations,* because they are, in their essence, inextricably wedded to the biases and orientation of their translators. I need not point out how a story, told to one person, who tells it to another, and so on, can bear no resemblance in the end to the original; some parts can become magnified, others exaggerated, and others omitted altogether.

A scholarly discussion of variations of translations is presented by Dr. Khaleel Mohammed in the *Middle East Quarterly*. Dr. Mohammed points out the various impositions of medievalists upon the vast majority of currently-available translations of the Koran – especially those most commonly distributed by Wahhabists and Salafists (another strain of repressive Islam). They rely, for example, on the interpretations of Yusuf Ali and Muhammad Khan. Dr. Mohammed states in "The Koran Interpreted," that Arthur Arberry (1905-69):

"... acknowledged the orthodox Muslim view that the Qu'ran cannot be translated, but only interpreted. He rendered the Qur'an into understandable English and separated text from tradition. The translation is without prejudice and is probably the best around."

Dr. Mohammed also notes that Muhammad Asad's translation of the Koran is notably "bucking the Saudi orthodoxy" and to its credit banned in Saudi Arabia. Any academic linguist can confirm that perfect translations of a text from one language to another can often be essentially impossible, especially when dealing with classical Arabic, which is the expertise of only a tiny minority of Muslims.

It is my belief that most lay Muslims have the capacity to understand the Koran or to find the innumerable resources which can – when put together by an individual, liberty-loving Muslim – give a more mainstream, pluralistic interpretation of passages that, until now, have remained solely in the province of Islamist "experts" to interpret, on their behalf.

Interpreting the Koran through the lens of freedom: History is not religion.

Well-intentioned scholars, non-Muslim critics of Islamism and Jihadism, and especially the Jihadists themselves, may differ on the version(s) of history that I was taught, and have conveyed herein.

Pious anti-Islamist Muslims will typically want to remain grounded in the integrity of our Arabic Koran while presenting an anti-Jihadist interpretation of the same scripture. *There can be no more*

effective weapon to defeat the militant Islamists. The only other option is a disassembly of Islam's Koranic history, which to most Muslims would make the faith unrecognizable. It is Muslims who love their faith, get close to God through reading their Koran, *and yet reject Islamism* who are the *only* ones with the credibility to put global militant Islamism into remission, on a local and global scale.

A simple reading of Chapter 9, Verse 5 above states, *"slay the idolators wherever you find them."* But this same violence, when done in self-defense, or after violation of a peace treaty in necessary self- preservation by a faith community on the verge of annihilation, can be an ethic which most would respect and stands against terrorism.

In 2007, it would be equally moral for a Muslim to say that we should *"slay al Qaeda wherever we find them."* Thus, a Muslim learns these passages as exhortations from God regarding war as last resort, and with the underpinning of principles of *just* war. These same principles have been used in other faiths to this very day, to justify war in the protection of our nation-states.

At the end of the day, what truly matters the most to the free world is not necessarily whose version of Arabian history from 610-632 C.E. is the "truth." What matters most is *whether the predominant Muslim version of that history in the 21st century being taught to our children is compatible with American and western morality of "just war," and post-modern enlightenment values of universal freedoms.*

If Muslims can begin to articulate and establish an ijtihad (reinterpretation of scripture in the light of modernity) through the lens of individual freedom, we can then reconcile our faith, our religion, with American ideology. We cannot surrender the mantle of our faith to the militant Islamists or the Jihadists. *Our Koranic passages are what Muslims make of them – not what extremists dictate to us.* It will remain what extremists dictate to us *only so long as we abrogate our duty to defeat their Islamist/Jihadist ideology and interpretations.*

As an American and as a Muslim, I have always been an admirer of Thomas Jefferson – especially his articulation of and respect for religious liberty. Above everything, Jefferson espoused a respect for liberty which Muslims need to lift up. He also laid out the challenge for liberty reformists:

"The generation which commences a revolution rarely completes it. Habituated from their infancy to passive submission of body and mind to their kings and priests, they are not qualified when called on to think and provide for themselves; and their inexperience, their ignorance and bigotry make them instruments often in the hands of the Bonapartes and Iturbides to defeat their own rights and purposes." --Thomas Jefferson to John Adams, 1823. ME 15:464

And at its crux, it is the Jeffersonian ethos that bin Laden in his latest video rant, stands so militantly against. Jefferson also said,

The legitimate powers of government extend to such acts only as are injurious to others. It does me no injury for my neighbor to say there are twenty gods or no god. It neither picks my pocket nor breaks my leg.

In the defense of freedom for all under God, Muslims need to wake-up to the current relative vacuum of reasoned Islamic theological defenses of liberty. Anti-Islamist Muslims are far behind where we should be in the theological defense of liberty.

Bin Laden understands freedom and free markets and its deep threat upon the power he seeks. In his latest screed, he reserved special condemnation for the economic manifestation of freedom – capitalism – the free exchange of privately-owned values among a free people. He castigated it as an evil ideology.

In part four, I will present an example of Jihad in Koranic scripture.

4

Which Islam? Whose Islam? Part 4 of 4

All Muslims Own the Interpretation of the Koran
September 14, 2007

An example of Jihad in the Koranic scripture

The organization of the Koran, as a full text, is not chronological, but rather, is believed by most Muslims to have been directed as to its chapter and verse to the Prophet Mohammed by the Angel Gabriel over the 22 and one-half years of revelation from God. The first Caliph, Abu Bakr, the closest companion of the Prophet Mohammed, first made the Koran into a single volume. It was then widely distributed by the Second Caliph, Omar. The organizational structure is from the longest chapter to shortest. While this organization can help maintain its theological authenticity, it also makes it easier for militant Islamists to dissociate history from religion, and try to extrapolate verses which originally applied only to a single conflict, towards a grossly distorted and inappropriate general call for war.

Within Chapters 2, 5, and 9 (in that chronological order) are various discussions concerning the Tribe of Quraysh, the original tribe of the Prophet Mohammed, based in Mecca. Many of the members of Quraysh remained idol-worshippers, and repeatedly persecuted and warred with those who had left the tribe to become Muslims. In fact, the Muslim calendar begins in the year of emigration away from Mecca, toward Medina.

> *They ask you about the lunar months, say these are timing devices for people and for pilgrimage. It is not piety to come to the houses from the back of them; but piety is to be godfearing; so come to the houses by their doors, and fear God; so that you may succeed. (2:189) And fight in the way of God with those who fight you, but aggress not: God loves not the aggressors. (Koran 2:190) Kill them anywhere you find them and push them out from where they pushed you out, persecution is more grievous than slaying. Do not fight them in the Holy Mosque until they fight you there; then if they fight you, slay them- such is the consequences for the unbelievers who fight you. (Koran 2:191) But if they desist, surely god is All-forgiving, all-compassionate. (Koran 2:192)*

Idol-worshipping was rampant in Mecca. The Ka'ba was the home of hundreds of idols prior to Islam.

Mohammed began to receive the revelation of Islam from the Angel Gabriel in 610 C.E. Muslims who followed his monotheistic message, and belief in the God of Abraham, were persecuted and tortured for their views. They were viewed as a religious and economic threat to the polytheists. Pilgrimages into Mecca were a major source of income to those who facilitated and aided it, and Islam was threatening that monopoly. In 615 C.E., Muslims escaped to Abyssinia (Ethiopia) for their own safety, but then returned. Similarly, they later emigrated from Mecca to Medina, in 622 C.E. They were invited by the leaders of Yathrib (Medina) to help broker a peace among the various tribes in conflict in Medina.

Muslims fought the Meccans in three major battles and in a number of skirmishes over the years of Mohammed's proclamations after arriving in Yathrib (Medina). The Muslims of Medina were able to maintain their position and avoid defeat. With the ongoing threat of further battles, in 628 C.E., Mohammed led Muslims back to Mecca, to immigrate back to their homeland. War was averted through the signing of the ten-year peace treaty of Hudabiyah, between the Muslims and the Meccans. In exchange for being allowed to complete their yearly pilgrimage to Mecca, the Muslims agreed to stay in Medina all other times of the year, and to never proselytize their faith. Muslims believe that the above verses (2:190-192) were revealed in answer to a concern over what they would do if they were attacked by the Meccans, while doing their rituals in Mecca.

Thus, to a peaceful Muslim, this passage has nothing to do with aggressively killing *anyone*, let alone Christians and Jews. It is, rather, about Muslims being given permission to defend themselves, and to enter a just war *only* if and when the treaty they had signed was violated by the idol-worshippers of the Quraysh tribe in Mecca.

According to this interpretation, then, war was thus the consequence of a violation of a signed treaty, and *only* as a last resort. It also must be done justly, and end immediately if the enemy disengages from the conflict. The instructions given to our American soldiers fighting al Qaeda and other militant Islamists today are no different, in principle. Certainly, this is not to compare what was in essence a theocracy at the formation of the first Islamic state, with our own free, secular American society.

The climate of violent, immoral Arab tribes which existed just prior to the revelation of Islam is also a far more medieval society than our own. However, the morals and principles our leaders may rely upon in order to justly enter armed conflict are similar. Thus, the murderous violation of peace treaties, confiscation of property, and commission of torture and mayhem between tribes can only be responded to with war that is based in justice and humanitarianism. As history has repeatedly seen, without God's guidance permitting armed response, *"to turn the other cheek"* would have meant the annihilation of the Muslim population. Just as the God of Abraham sanctioned Moses to engage in war to defend the Jewish people against the idol-worshippers, so too do Muslims believe that Mohammed was divinely authorized to defend Muslims through war.

The reformation process to defeat Islamism and Jihadism in the 21st century will need to relegate to history the example of Mohammed – which conflated all of his roles as spiritual leader, faith leader, and governmental and military leader.

Today, Muslims can and must separate history and religion. The verses that Jihadists and Islamists often cite as justification relate to a very specific battle in ancient Muslim history, and in the context of the war that erupted from the tribal conflicts and persecution of Muslims, between the Meccan idol- worshipping tribe of Quraysh, and the Muslims of Medina. Within these stories and history are principles of just warfare: that is, one that is based in self-defense, only fighting against those who attacked first, and admonitions to only fight as much as is absolutely necessary to secure an enduring peace.

Nowhere in the Koran does God tell Muslims how to establish and run their governments. Nowhere in the

Koran does God tell Muslims that they must emulate the Prophet Mohammed's role and actions as a military or governmental leader. Nowhere in the Koran does God tell Muslims that they must impose their beliefs, practices and rituals upon others. And most certainly, nowhere in the Koran does God tell myopic automatons to instigate murderous, terrorist actions against civilians and other non- combatants who, by definition, are incapable of causing them harm.

My interpretation of the Koran has always included the overriding idea that the Prophet Mohammed's example, spiritually and morally, is for all times – but that his political and military actions were an example that cannot be taken out of the context of the times in which he lived.

As contemporary Muslims, we need to relegate to history the fact that the origins of our faith were established by a fighting force that defended a faith-community that was also a nation-state, 1,400 years ago. We need to acknowledge that a nation like the United States with its Constitution written atop natural laws, where our faith's rules are our own to practice, in a secular, individual and peaceful fashion, is far preferable to living under a theocracy – Islamic or otherwise – in which one faith, and only that faith, may be practiced as enforced by threats, coercion and violence.

Thus, verse 2:190 refers to the tribe of Quraysh, and cannot be extrapolated to any other group to justify war. Similarly, verse (2:191) refers to the earlier time in which the Muslims had been removed from their homes in Mecca prior to emigrating to Medina.

With this interpretation of these verses, one could make an argument that Islam advocates peace, and only condones war *as a last resort,* as a *defensive* measure, against annihilation. I and other liberty- loving Muslims wholeheartedly reject the notion that this verse can be interpreted to justify commandeering airplanes, murdering their flight crews, and flying them into buildings occupied by innocent civilians. Similarly, I reject the entire notion that this passage can be used to justify the imposition of Islamism – or even Islam itself – upon anyone through any means, least of all through violent, offensive warfare. Further, liberty-loving minded Muslims will stand against Islamism as a political ideology, and will do everything in our power to prevent its metastasizing through our culture.

One of the most frequently-cited Koranic passages by militant Islamists and Jihadists is Chapter 9, Verse 5. The literal interpretation of the series of verses (9:4-9:7), from sources I have always used, is as follows:

> *Those of the unbelievers (idol-worshippers) who signed treaties with you and did not violate them, provided*

no assistance to your enemies, and abided by their commitments to you, then by all means keep your commitments to them, God loves the God-fearing who keep their word. (9:4) Then, when the sacred months are drawn away, slay the idolators (those who did not sign treaties) wherever you find them, and confine them, and lie in wait for them at every place. But, if they repent and establish worship, and practice charity, let them go their way, God is all-forgiving, all compassionate. (9:5) If an unbeliever (idolator) requests an asylum with you, grant it to him, so he may have the chance of hearing the word of God, then convey him to his place of security. That is because they are a people who do not know. (9:6) The idol-worshippers have no credibility with God or His apostle, but as to those who made the treaty with you at the Grand Mosque, honor it with you. God loves those who abide by what they promise. (9:7)

This passage also refers to the "disbelievers," which refers only to the idol-worshippers of Quraysh, at that particular time in Muslim history when the Meccans were looking to destroy the Muslims, and then violated the treaty they had signed. After the violation, Muslims threatened war but came into Mecca peacefully by promising that if their enemies stayed in their homes, there would be no war.

Thus, war was averted. War ethic teaches that a

diplomatic threat of war can be necessary in order to prevent war. This passage also only refers to the idol-worshippers of Mecca, and no other faith group at all, and no other time in history.

Freedom-loving Muslims must help America and the free world fight against Islamists and Jihadists. The only way for Islamists to abort their dream of a theocracy under their version of Islam is for them to be overwhelmed with a better vision (interpretation) of an Islam and our Koran based in liberty: an Islam that articulates and defends pluralism, tolerance, free speech, free markets, and all the other fruits of a free society; an Islam that rests at home with the freedoms which Americans claim as their birthright and will defend at all costs.

5

Understanding the Cauldron that Brewed ISIS

Religious Freedom Institute
July 12, 2016

Religious communities in Iraq, especially religious minorities, have suffered enormously over the past year. Longstanding sectarian tensions between Shiites and Sunnis deepen the crisis in Iraq, which is disrupting the entire Middle East. This week contributors are asked to evaluate this situation as a crisis of religious freedom. They address the following questions:

> *What explains the success of ISIS in Iraq?*
> *Why do sectarian tensions exist?*
>
> *What can be done to resolve this conflict and prevent similar ones in the future?*
> *What role might US or international religious freedom diplomacy play?*

Part 1: Historical Context

The plight of religious minorities, particularly Christians and Yazidis, in Iraq has the world asking: *How did a land where Christianity existed for millennia become the world's most dangerous place for Christians and other minority faiths?*

The spread and growth of the Islamic State in Iraq and al-Sham (Levant) (ISIS) has placed the existence of Christian and Yazidi faithful and other minorities at risk like never before. Yet, ISIS did not come out of thin air. It is the result of a perfect storm—the 50-year trajectory of historical, political, and sectarian religious forces in both Syria and Iraq meeting the wake of the ongoing Syrian Revolution. Understanding the evolution of ISIS as a byproduct of Syrian tyranny, the revolution, and Iranian imperialism in the region helps to explain ISIS's success in Iraq and Syria and reveals possible long-term solutions.

As the son of Syrian immigrants, political refugees from the prison Syria became in the early 1960s under the Ba'athist Party regime, my lens for the horrors of the Syrian conflict is particularly personal and palpable. Almost every day we communicate with family living in fear in Aleppo and Damascus.

The Syrian Ba'ath Party, an Arab nationalist socialist party, seized power by military coup in 1963. The Alawite (a Shi'a offshoot) faction of Ba'ath Party loyalists then took power in another bloody coup in February 1966. After the Alawite coup of 1966, the fascist Ba'ath Party transformed its predominantly supremacist political platform to incorporate Alawite religious sectarianism. Members of Sunni Muslim leadership were purged from the military. The entire leadership became comprised of Alawite Ba'athist faithful. Sunni, Christian, Druze, and Islamaili influence was all but eliminated. Non-Alawite officers who were ousted reported that in the late 1960s and early '70s Syria was on the verge of a sectarian civil war.

But, in 1970, Hafez al-Assad took the reins from his fellow Alawites in another coup. Assad, in line with the totalitarian doctrine of the Ba'athist Party, ruled Syria with an iron fist for 30 years. Al-Assad ended the Ba'ath Alawite in-fighting and the regime cleansed any non-Alawites in its midst, obliterating any Sunni protestations within or outside the party. To quell religious sectarian unrest, Assad placed a few party loyalists who were Sunni, Christian, and Druze in mid-level and a few higher levels of political, but not military, leadership, though most knew them to be window dressing and sympathizers.

The Syria of Hafez Assad was much like the Iraq of Ba'athist Saddam Hussein, described by a pseudonymous expatriate as "A Republic of Fear": "a regime of totalitarian rule, institutionalized violence, universal fear, and unchecked personal dictatorship." Many of our Syrian families, after suffering for years in and out of prison, muzzled in every form of expression left for American freedom after realizing that a revolution to topple one of the world's most ruthless military tyrannies would likely never materialize in their lifetimes.

The Assad regime paralyzed the humanity of 22 million Syrians for two generations using incalculably cruel methods. Brothers, sisters, families reported on one another to Syrian intelligence (Mukhabarat); many vanished, never to be seen again; and anyone who dared dissent from the ruling party was systematically tortured and made an example with frequent collective punishment. By the twenty-first century, there would come to be more Syrians living outside Syria than inside, and some analyses claim that one in nine expatriates living abroad provided steady information to the Assad regime on expatriate Syrian activities in order to spare family. The Syrian Human Rights Committee (http://www.shrc.org/) has chronicled many of the atrocities committed in the past 45 years by the Assad regime: the Hama Massacres of 1963, 1982, and again in 2011, Tadmur, and the countless prisoners of conscience systematically snuffed out by the regime.

Although the Assad regime tolerated some religious difference where it did not interfere with political objectives, that meager toleration began to deteriorate into the religious catastrophe that has characterized the Syrian Revolution as a result of two key factors.

First, in the 1980s the secular Alawite Ba'athist party began a deep alliance with theocratic, Khomeinist Iran. The Assad regime came under the monolithic influence of a Shi'a crescent from Iran to Syria and Lebanon (vis-à-vis Hizballah). Syria helped Iran in the bloody Iraq-Iran war and, especially after Bashar al-Assad's 2000 ascent to power, began a major increase in economic, military and cultural cooperation with Iran. With Iran came it's anti-Christian, anti-Semitic, and anti-Sunni ideology. Iran's Khomeinist regime (http://www.uscirf.gov/countries/iran) is not only one of the world's worst offenders of religious freedom but also sponsors Islamist terrorism, including progeny terror groups like Hizballah. Its own theocratic version of Shi'a Islam is a militant misogynistic supremacist version of Shi'a Islamism. The Alawites were all too willing to allow this intolerant influence to permeate Syrian culture. Assadist Ba'athists maintained military and governmental control, letting Khomeinists infiltrate the nation.

Second, the Assad regime's brewing intolerance mirrored regional militant Sunni Islamist ideologies from Saudi Arabia (Wahhabism), Syria, Egypt, Jordan, and Qatar (Muslim Brotherhood (MB)). Due to Islamist media dominance, and the departure of liberal refugees the ideological trajectory of Syria's Sunni population was also increasingly fundamentalist. Nothing illustrates this systemic radicalization campaign better than how Assad maintained close relations with the Iranian backed terror group Hizballah and its leader Sheikh Hassan Nasrallah while also providing sanctuary for the exiled leadership of the Sunni terror group HAMAS (an MB offshoot) and its leader Khaled Mashal until almost a year after the revolution started.

When the Arab Awakening and revolution came to Syria in 2012, these two radicalizing currents, which affected both Shi'a and Sunni Muslims, created fertile ground for sectarian violence and the growth of ISIS in both Syria and Iraq.

Part 2: Contemporary Problems and Solutions

In March 2011, the Arab Awakening came to Syria, bringing a long overdue opportunity for reform. But the vacuum it created skyrocketed the influence of both Shi'a and Sunni regional Islamist movements. Minorities like Christians were increasingly caught in the middle 2025%20hearing%20final.pdf) of the bloody crossfire between Shi'a and Sunni Islamists and secular Ba'athists, working hand in glove with the Shi'a Islamists.

This cauldron of political repression and sectarian conflict was set afire with the revolution of 2011 in

Syria. Yet, the revolution began in rural Syria in towns like Dar'aa as a predominantly secular, political pluralistic revolt united against Assadist, Ba'athist tyranny. Initially few religious freedom issues surfaced.

But in 2012 the conflict collapsed into its sectarian roots as unarmed civilians were massacred in the streets, in their homes and at work by barrel bombs, chemical weapons, helicopter gunships and raiding gangs (shabiha) who savaged neighborhoods, torturing, raping, murdering, and imprisoning, and leaving over 100,000 dead and 1 million displaced.

The regime had adopted a strategy of "divide and conquer," exploiting sectarianism, and as the conflict developed in 2012, this strategy began to work. The government released thousands of militant Sunni Islamists from jails. Large numbers of radical foreign Sunni jihadists started to flow into Syria, and their Shi'a equivalent, Hizballah Shi'a jihadists, arrived to fight alongside the Syrian military.

As a result, the Free Syria Army (FSA) found themselves no longer up against the regime alone, but fighting an emerging battle on many fronts against Assad's military and factions of militant Islamists—a situation that smashed the fighting resolve of minority groups like Christians, Druze, and anti-Ba'athist Alawites.

This process allowed the formation, growth, and militarization of ISIS in northeast Syria. The "moderate" (non-Islamist) wings of the FSA steered clear of the ISIS fanatics and focused on defeating the Syrian military. ISIS, conversely, left the Syrian military virtually alone as they viewed their initial existential enemy to be moderate Sunni Muslims who would reject their Islamist supremacism and authority. Similarly, the Assad military left ISIS virtually alon the *Wall Street Journal* described it as an entente) as their continued existence gave the Syrian military a way to rally global sentiment against the revolution while they decimated the greatest existential threat to Assadist Ba'athism and its alliance with Iranian Khomenism: moderate democratic-minded Sunni Muslims. So, while ISIS grew, the genocide against Sunni Muslims continued. The conflict in Syria has now left over 250,000 dead and 5 million displaced, 90 percent of whom are Sunni Muslim.

Systematic savagery by the Syrian regime against predominantly Sunni Muslims and selective Saudi and Qatari funding of radical Islamist wings of the FSA fueled an unprecedented Sunni radicalization. While the FSA and Syrian government were both shrinking in size and power, ISIS was the only growing entity in Syria. ISIS continued to grow faster and was able to spread to Iraq, dissolving "secular" borders and claiming a caliphate under Sheikh Abu Bakr al-Baghdadi. Few predicted how significant the ability of radical Islamist movements like ISIS would be to fill the vacuum created in Syria.

ISIS has created, in areas it controls, the world's most horrific situation for religious minorities like Yazidis, Christians, Assyrians, Kaldeans, and Druze. These minorities, as well as dissenting Sunnis, are systematically tortured, raped, and murdered. Their sacred holy places and sacred texts, symbols, and history are destroyed and their worship practices prohibited.

Solving the religious freedom catastrophe in Syria and Iraq must be viewed through the lens exactly how ISIS emerged. ISIS is an unhinged outgrowth of militant Islamism manifest directly from Wahhabism and various forms of Salafism throughout the Arab world but especially Saudi Arabia (http://www.uscirf.gov/countries/saudi-arabia). The growth of ISIS is a result of a perfect storm of, first, a genocidal Syrian government, second the radicalization of Sunni Muslims in Syria and Iraq, and third an Iraqi government incapable of mounting strong resistance to ISIS.

This analysis teaches that the only solution is a military one, which ends both ISIS and the Assad regime. They are two sides, Sunni and Shi'a, of the same radicalizing coin, feeding off of sectarian animus and divisions. The only option that may restore a nation that before the revolution had the most diverse population in the Middle East is a post-Ba'ath, post-ISIS Syria. ISIS cannot be defeated in Iraq without decisively destroying their command and control in Northeast Syria in and around Raqqa. And the decimation of ISIS alone will only delay the formation of another radical Islamist group if the Assad military remains intact and in place.

Make no mistake: The fact that long before the Arab Awakening there were virtually no Jews remaining in Arab nations speaks volumes to the disastrous trajectory of religious freedom in the Middle East. The population of Christians in Iraq, too, has declined precipitously as so-called secular regimes became closely aligned with radical Islam.

Saddam Hussein "relocated" Christian communities and oversaw an almost 50 percent decrease in the Iraqi Christian population from 1.4 million in 1987 to 800,000 in 2003. Since then, with Ba'athism and Islamism cornering minorities, the number of Christians in Iraq has decreased to 300,000. The population is plummeting again in Iraq and Syria as ISIS marks their homes for genocide with "N" for Nazarene.

The only way for religious freedom, the first freedom, to find life in Iraq and Syria is for the revolution against the twin tyrannies of Assadist Ba'athism and ISIS' Islamism to be realized. Things will get worse before getting better, but to deny the need for revolution against tyranny is to accept the return of a false quiet. In the last 50 years many perceived a period of quiet for religious sectarian animus. Really, a period of mass imprisonment, and sectarian monopoly was festering in a cauldron of religious divisions. The Assad regime used those divisions to justify its brutality in a cycle that must end if genuine religious freedom is to have any hope in Syria or Iraq. And countering the social media recruitment of ISIS jihadis around the planet is not enough. We need a program of positive messaging from Muslims for religious liberty in addition to that against religious extremism and supremacism. Urgency is essential: If the religious diversity of Syria is lost, so too will be its greatest hope of emerging from this horrific battle between the savagery of radical Sunni and Shi'a Islamists and the Assad Ba'athist killing machine.

The opinions expressed here are the author's own and do not reflect the views of his organization.

.

6

A Muslim Reformer Explains How to Fight Islamism

The Federalist
July 13, 2017

'For the West to see a day free from wars against Islamist terror…we must wage an ideological war to influence the minds of Muslims,' says Zuhdi Jasser.

Dr. M. Zuhdi Jasser is president and founder of the American Islamic Forum for Democracy (AIFD), co-founder of the Muslim Reform Movement (MRM), and author of "A Battle for the Soul of Islam: An American Muslim Patriot's Fight to Save His Faith." He is a practicing Muslim who has actively opposed Islamism.

Jasser is an active physician and former U.S. Navy officer whose parents fled Syria in the 1960s, and host of the Blaze Radio Podcast "Reform This!" and founder of

TakeBackIslam.com.

The author interviewed him in January on the Muslim Reform Movement, Islamism, and the war in Syria. This is a follow-up interview. Jasser agreed to discuss Islamism and searching for its antidote in the United Kingdom, the United States, and the Middle East.

Lessons from London

Q (Postal): As a co-founder of the Muslim Reform Movement, what lessons do you want the West to learn from the recent terrorist attacks in the United Kingdom?

A (Jasser): We in the free world cannot ever afford to be complacent. Military victories in Iraq and Syria will increase ISIS' global chatter calling for acts of war against the West and subsequent attempts at more attacks will follow. The emergence of ISIS in 2013 after the diminishment of al-Qaeda by 2008 should serve as a reminder that we are in a long global war against militant Islamism, and more broadly non-violent Islamism.

The precursor of violent Islamism and violent jihad is non-violent Islamism and its civilizational jihad. Islamists of any variety divide the world into the "Land of Islam" (Dar-al-Islam) and the "Land of War" (Dar al-Harb).

Islamists will continue to promote the consciousness that non-Muslim majority nations are the "Land of War."

Nearly every one of these attacks is following the same pattern and we should learn from them. Sadly, we are not. The perpetrators over and over prove to be "*known* wolves" (radicals *already* on the radar of security apparatuses). The concept of a "lone wolf" is a fictitious construct absolving non-violent Islamists of any responsibility.

Islamists know that the greatest threat to their supremacist program is when we advance the ideas of liberty, freedom, and universal values of human rights protected by secular national identity. That is the only antidote to Islamism (political Islam and the idea of an Islamic state). The means of terror has now morphed from suicide belts and bombs to vehicular jihad and machetes. While we must learn to confront this changing landscape, we must see all these attacks for what they are: the very tip of the iceberg, the militant violent expressions of the massive global Islamist movement.

We can and will continue to fight this war in Afghanistan, Pakistan, Syria, Iraq, Yemen and Libya. But victories there are only pyrrhic and fleeting. In order for the West to see a day free from wars against Islamist terror and its caliphate(s), we must wage an ideological war to influence the minds of Muslims against political Islam.

Muslim reformers have a laboratory here in the West to dissect theocratic Islam in ways that just cannot be done in any Muslim-majority nation. We, for example, reached out with a plea to Ariana Grande for her to use her enormous cultural platform of millions to empower Muslim reformers to become ambassadors of freedom, gender equality, sexual identity, free speech and all the issues that distinguish us from Islamist societies and their sharia states. Unfortunately, her One Love benefit concert was another in a long history of lost opportunities.

> *Q: One of the London bridge terrorists (Khuram Butt) reportedly viewed sermons online by Ahmad Musa Jibril, an Islamist preacher in Dearborn, Michigan, who praises violent jihad. Butt also allegedly associated with Islamist preacher Anjem Choudary, who is set to be released from prison next year after calling for British Muslims to support ISIS in 2013. (You called for his arrest seven years ago). How should U.S. and U.K. authorities, and Muslim communities in those countries, deal with Islamist websites, preachers, and mosques in the future?*

A: Essentially, once homeland security agents finally shift their focus to "Countering Violent Islamism" (CVI) all Islamist groups and individuals can be rightfully viewed by authorities as possible cultivators of violent Islamism.

Individuals are not "radicalized" on the Internet. Their ideas are brewed in a local cauldron of Islamism that then drives them towards further Islamism and jihadism.

The Internet is merely a tool for the already radicalized Islamist. Islamist ideas include antipathy for Western society, governments, military, and foreign policy. Islamists are misogynists and anti-Semites. They obsess with conspiracy theories and condition Muslims to always be victims and bear grievances against non-Muslims. Islamist grievance groups in the West, such as most Muslim Brotherhood legacy groups, are the first steps in Muslim radicalization.

Authorities should closely monitor Islamist speech short of advocacy of violence and war against the West, in addition to obviously treasonous speech advocated by clerics like Anjem Choudary. Authorities shouldn't evaluate those who have traveled abroad or are connected to known militants in a vacuum, but rather drill down on the ideological adherence to elements of the Islamist movement.

We should also, however, not fall prey to the autocratic inclination of just shutting down non-violent Islamist and jihadi-sympathizing mosques. Rather, our entire security apparatus domestically (DHS) and abroad (DOD and State) should be mapping and monitoring their *public* (not private) footprints. Our Muslim Reform Movement's declaration is an ideological firewall that can be used to determine which Muslim groups are part of the problem and which Muslim groups are part of the solution.

> *Q: The United Kingdom is monitoring up to 23,000 Islamists as "subjects of interest," and yet Khuram Butt, the Manchester terrorist (Salman Abedi) and the Westminster terrorist (Khalid Masood) were able to successfully carry out attacks despite being previously monitored or investigated. What can the United States learn from this to prevent further attacks? How should the United States deal with its "known wolves," as you like to call them?*

A: The central axis upon which our homeland security focus is currently centered is labeled "CVE: Countering Violent Extremism." Thus, our agents are not told or encouraged to focus on obvious precursor Islamist ideologies to that violence but rather somehow they are supposed to focus on the moment some non-descript extremism becomes violent. This is impossible, as our agents hamstring themselves waiting for that virtual needle in a haystack.

In the United Kingdom, they are following 23,000 suspects looking for both a confirmed predilection for violence and also an imminent threat. A security strategy that only focuses on behavior will fail over and over as we have seen. Many so-called "violent extremists" have no violent precursors, but Islamist extremists always have Islamist precursors. Thus, we need to shift from a focus simply upon those imminently planning acts of violence (terror) upon citizens to focusing upon those harboring the precursor ideology of non-violent Islamism. The axis of DHS security work should center on CVI (Countering Violent Islamism), not CVE.

Domestic Developments

This doesn't mean that Muslim citizens should have their civil rights compromised. We should focus on Islamist public messaging and adherents. The monitoring of the readily available public footprint of non-violent Islamists should be a matter of routine surveillance. Authorities do not need warrants for this type of surveillance, and our agents should be using the Islamist nature of those posts to narrow down their threat risk.

> *Q: On your Twitter feed dated July 6, you remarked that Linda Sarsour, in a speech to ISNA (Islamic Society of North America) delivered over Independence Day weekend, called for a "jihad" against President Trump and praised Siraj Wahhaj, who in a conversation with you highlighted in your book called for the overthrow of the U.S. Constitution by the Qur'an. In that same speech, Sarsour also called for Muslims to refuse to*

assimilate into the United States. How should Muslim reformers and their non-Muslims allies best respond to her speech?

A: Sarsour's jihadi comments and the flurry of public outrage may be the beginning of thought leaders in the West seeking out Muslim reformers as a response to the jihadism of Islamists like Sarsour. There will always be droves of useful idiots like Abigail Abrams at *Time* who hysterically try to apologize for the likes of Sarsour, who lead the radicalization of Muslims against America and secular liberal democracies.

But the jihadi Sarsours of the world will remain as "the" voice of Islam and Muslims if Muslim reformers are not given equal time on all forms of media to counter and marginalize her radicalization. As you point out, I have been exposing her mentor's radicalism since I reported Siraj Wahhaj's 1995 call for the overthrow of our U.S. Constitution at the same annual ISNA convention. It's time for Americans to connect the dots between ISIS operatives, Middle Eastern sharia states, and these American Islamist thought leaders. Only we reformers at the Muslim Reform Movement can begin the process of putting violent jihad and its global Islamist movement into the dustbin of history.

Sadly, Sarsour's speech is one among thousands of speeches and sermons delivered every day by leading

Islamists in the West. Only bigger platforms by Muslim reformers can counter that very real jihad. As I've said many times, the only jihad we need is a "jihad against jihad."

> *Q: What is your opinion on the Trump administration's travel ban against six Muslim-majority nations? Would you advise President Trump any differently on this in the wake of the recent terrorist in the United Kingdom?*

A: The travel pause, not an actual ban, is a necessary initial tool for the commander-in- chief to reset the vetting mechanism of those seeking the privilege of entering our country. Yes, it's true that most attacks on the homeland have been homegrown Islamist threats and not refugees. Yes, the nations with the greatest ideological threats like Saudi Arabia, Egypt, Qatar, and Pakistan were not included in the ban.

But that doesn't invalidate the legitimacy of a pause on refugee immigration. The pause is simply the beginning of a shift toward a more rigorous form of vetting that I hope will include screening of Islamist ideologies.

Some studies report around 23 percent of those seeking refuge here have sympathies for ISIS. Those individuals have no right to come to the United States. Those who come to the United States should not do so solely out of humanitarian need, but also to share our values. Those with sympathies for Islamists (e.g., Muslim Brotherhood or ISIS) as well as those with sympathies for fascist dictatorships (e.g., Assadists or those with allegiances to the Russian government) should never be given the freedom to come to the U.S.

The nations included in the travel pause are at best not even allies and at worst our enemies and virtual anarchies on the verge of collapse. It makes perfect sense to identify anyone coming from those nations as needing extra vetting. There is nothing discriminatory against vetting people who happen to come from these specific countries, even if they are predominantly Muslim.

My advice to President Trump is that he assemble his campaign-promised "Commission on Radical Islamism" and have that commission become the focal point of our domestic and foreign policy shift away from CVE toward Countering Violent Islamism. It needs to have a heavy presence of reformist American Muslims in order to deflect commonplace attacks from Islamist identity groups that the commission would be "anti-Muslim." There is nothing more pro-Muslim and pro-Islam than engaging Muslims and non-Muslims in a campaign to marginalize and defeat the Islamist theocrats in our communities.

> *Q: In our previous interview, you discussed the differences between Muslim reformers and Muslim Islamists. You recently called Daily Beast author Dean Obeidallah a*

"non-violent Islamist." What do you mean by this?

A: Dean has been raising money for and defending Islamist groups like CAIR (Council on American Islamic Relations) and ISNA (Islamic Society of North America) for over a decade. Contrary to his useful idiots, he doesn't have an excuse of being unaware of the realities of sharia supremacism taught and indoctrinated from the books and teachings of many if not most American and Western mosques.

He is a Muslim attorney who under the false and obnoxious cloak of comedy provides cover for droves of Islamists, and actively leads fundraisers for their movements in the West every month. He is particularly dangerous in that his comedic shtick and focus on grievances mainstreams his apologetics for Islamism and in fact starts many on the path of anti-American radicalization.

His Islamist bona fides are evidenced by his pathological silence when it comes to the identifying or acknowledging that the Islamist platform of ideas is always the precursor of militant Islamism. If the Ikhwan (Muslim Brotherhood) movement were not covert in the West, they would likely proudly award him one of their leading awards for defense and advocacy.

Q: What is your opinion about the recent protests against Sharia law in the United States? Do you think these protests are a legitimate form of criticism against Islamism, or do they express bigotry against Muslims?

A: When Muslims protested the sharia state of the Muslim Brotherhood in Egypt in 2013, that was not anti-Muslim bigotry. When the Green Revolution protested the Khomenist sharia state of Iran, that was not anti-Muslim, and when judges and lawyers in Pakistan protested the sharia state of Pakistan that was not anti-Muslim. Those are only a few examples. In fact, it is very pro-Muslim to reject theocratic Islamism and their instrument of their Islamist interpretations and institutionalization of sharia.

First, and foremost, every citizen should have a right to criticize any and all forms of sharia. That is part and parcel of genuine free speech. Anything short is the imposition of blasphemy laws. Many U.S. citizens are concerned when observing little to no condemnation from American Muslims as well as our anesthetized mainstream media of any of the draconian interpretations of sharia law which predominate the texts and teachings of most global Muslim institutions, including in the U.S.

My primary criticism of the rallies was simply that it just seemed a little odd that non-Muslims were rallying in cities across America, protesting to predominantly non-Muslim communities about the problems with the sharia law of Islamists. I would have rather seen their anti-sharia protests target the Organization of Islamic Cooperation

(OIC) and all of its attendant 56 Muslim majority nations who are the world's primary cauldrons of Islamist sharia law. The protests should have begun in front of the Saudi, Turkish, Qatari, Egyptian, and Pakistani embassies in Washington, to name a few.

Without identifying the sharia institutions they were protesting, I could not see what the point of the rallies were. If it was simply to educate the American public that sharia is the primary instrument of Islamism, then what are the next steps? What is the cure to that diagnosis? Is their goal to engage reformist Muslims? These rallies didn't even begin to accomplish that.

The Global Fight Against Islamism

Q: You recently criticized President Trump's speech in Saudi Arabia to Muslim nations in May, where he called on these Muslim nations to "drive out the terrorists." In this critique, you stated that this call was a "[g]reat sound bite," but that "the hall should have then almost emptied except for Tunisia, Indonesia and a few others," as "these tyrants [are] living off [of]...theocratic Islamist ideology that creates...global Islamist militants and their viral movements." A recent article in the Boston Globe reported that Saudi Arabia is instrumental in spreading Wahhabism beyond the Arab world to Afghanistan, Pakistan, Bosnia, and Indonesia. How would you advise the Trump administration to act differently towards Saudi Arabia and our other Muslim allies?

A: This question is so important. We desperately need to distinguish our short-term military and diplomatic goals from our long-term goals in the region. Our short-term goals are obvious. First, we need to decimate ISIS and maintain a semblance of stability in the Middle East and North Africa.

Our long-term goals and policies should be to advocate for those who share our values and respect universal human rights. President Trump continued the old and tired policies of the U.S. shoring up our Sunni Arab ally axis to balance the region against the Shia axis of Iran, Iraq, and Syria bolstered by Russia. While this strategy would be fitting during the Cold War when we had a bigger global threat in the Soviets, the post-Arab Awakening landscape is quite different.

We need to acknowledge that shoring up so-called allies who don't share our values contributes to those governments' oppression of their own citizens, which is against our core values as Americans, and contributes to radicalizing those Muslims rather than liberating them from theocracy. These policies run counter to our global responsibility as the leaders of the free world and the ambassadors for all those who want to be free.

In the end, as messy as the route may be, America's interest is to help those who want to be free achieve that God-given right. This process may be fraught with steps backward. But history has shown that eventually freedom will prevail. Anything short is to betray our own values and treat Muslim majority nations with a bigotry of low expectations.

Q: Saudi Arabia, Egypt, and the United Arab Emirates have recently cut ties to Qatar because Qatar allegedly paid $1 billion ransom to Iran and an al-Qaeda affiliate to release kidnapped members of Qatar's royal family. What are your thoughts on this?

A: I am no fan of the Saudi, Egyptian, or Emirati dictatorships. But in the global war against Islamism, most roads lead to Qatar first as the primary cancer of global Islamist movements and the Muslim Brotherhood's networks. Their propaganda vis-à-vis *Al Jazeera* and other associated global Islamist media outlets and Qatari-purchased think tanks and universities have further operationalized and weaponized the Islamist movement.

There is little doubt that when it comes to the radicalization of Muslims globally through Brotherhood networks across the planet, Qatar is a leading antagonist and enemy of the free world. This began all the way back in 1961, when Qatar welcomed the leading radical Islamist icon and spiritual inspiration of the Muslim Brotherhood, Sheikh Yusuf Qaradawi, who escaped from Egypt. Qatar has never looked back since in their fealty for the Ikhwan.

The U.S. has facilitated this for generations thanks to Qatar's domestic lobby influence and the U.S. military base in Qatar that has long been that lobby's insurance policy. But the House of al-Thani overreached by seeking financial ties with and facilitation of Iran's global Khomeinist networks. The Qatari royal family has even formed relationships with the Taliban and Al Qaeda. So we need to call this out, and isolate Qatar for its duplicity.

That being said, the Saudis are not innocent. Nor are their hands clean with regards to the cancer known as the Muslim Brotherhood. For over 50 years the Saudis have also financed and helped spread the establishment of Muslim Brotherhood legacy thinkers and groups in the West. The Wahhabis and the Ikhwan share both a hate of Western liberal democracies and a dream of wanting to establish Islamic states and the caliphate. Their essential difference lies in that Wahhabis are simply corporate, top-down, "elitist" Islamists, while the Brotherhood are grassroots, populist Islamists. Both their interpretations of Islam are supremacist and theocratic.

In the past few years things appear to be changing

somewhat. The century-old Islamist Sunni battle between the Saudi Wahhabis and the Ikhwan is now becoming more globalized likely due to Saudi Arabia's realized need to contain Qatar. At least in the short-term, the U.S. can leverage this to its advantage.

But in the long-term, we need to eventually stop policies of balancing tyrannies to establish an illusion of stability. We must isolate these entrenched tyrannies and cut off their lifelines to the world. There is no better place to start than Qatar and the Brotherhood network that it funds. However, I hope that this is the first phase of a longer process which will eventually lead to the isolation of Saudi Arabia and its global propagation of draconian Wahhabism.

Q: Recent reports have stated that days after the Trump administration criticized Qatar for funding terrorism, it authorized the sale of $12 billion in 36 F-15QA fighter jets to Qatar. What is your opinion on this?

A: This is hardly a way to "isolate" Qatar. It is time to end instances where the military (through bases, attachés, and congressionally approved arms sales), intelligence agents (CIA), State Department (diplomats), and the executive branch (president and U.N. ambassador) are all sending contradictory messages. Such contradictions give tyrants like the Al-Thani family of Qatar little motivation to ultimately change their behavior.

We should remember that the weapons which we sell them, with the intention of helping them maintain regional stability, are also used to shore up the government's domestic iron fist against their own citizens. In the end, we need to follow this recalibration of messaging and policies towards Qatar with a similar one with other "allies" like Saudi Arabia and other tyrannies to whom we supply arms, and from whom we buy oil.

Q: The Islamic State recently claimed responsibility for two attacks on Iran. Is this a significant development to you?

A: This is a very significant development for a number of reasons. First, any operation inside Iran, let alone Tehran, is obviously not easy to execute for Arabic-speaking Sunni Islamists: so few if any have ever been reported despite ISIS' deep animus with Shia Iran. Yet it appears that ISIS operatives were able to penetrate deep into the center of Farsi- speaking Tehran and target the symbolic sites of the parliament and the tomb of Ayatollah Khomeini, the symbol of the 1979 ascendancy of the Shia Khomeinist regime.

The primary nexus between Iran and ISIS are Iran's Arab allies in Syria and Iraq. So it is very likely that this operation was planned long in advance and involved a deep infiltration of the Iranian forces with covert ISIS operatives. It is very likely that ISIS operatives exploited

Iran's alliances with Arab-speaking Shia Islamist Iraqis and Alawite Syrians.

While ISIS may be on the run militarily in their strongholds of northern Iraq and Raqqa, Syria, this operation should illustrate their ability to continue to launch sophisticated global operations. This sophistication is great marketing for ISIS as the primary brand of radical Sunni Islamism, which will in turn yield many more jihadis against Iran, Assad, Hezbollah, and the West.

Particularly telling is that Amaq (the ISIS news agency) immediately released a video of their operatives yelling in Arabic "We are not leaving; we will remain, God willing." This was uploaded within minutes following the attacks in Tehran, and then released globally by ISIS. The phrase intentionally mimicked what ISIS spokesperson Mohammed Adnani said prior to his assassination in Syria.

The timing of this attack was likely in response to ISIS fearing a more unified West-Sunni front against them. ISIS likely wanted to deflect attention away from synergy between the West and Sunnis towards triggering a greater Sunni-Shia war. Exactly to this effect, Tehran immediately publicly blamed the attack on Riyadh, not ISIS.

Steve Postal works in health care policy in Washington DC.

7

Why A "Ritual Nick" Is a Smoke Screen for Female Genital Mutilation

The AHA Foundation
May 18, 2018

Any cutting or prick upon a female's genitalia that is not actually, absolutely medically necessary, but rather demanded by twisted interpretation of religion and misogynistic manifestations of culture, is abuse.

A "nick or cut" to the clitoral hood is not as benign as apologists who falsely wrap themselves in religious freedom would have you believe. The clitoral hood protects the glans of the clitoris, covers its shaft, and forms part of the structure of the labia minora.

Even if, one were to submit that the medical part of the procedure could possibly be done with no physical trauma (and that is a big fictitious 'if'), the whole intent of the procedure is ceremonially to desexualize women and place their bodies under patriarchal control.

The clitoral hood serves protective, immunological, and erogenous purposes. Cutting of the clitoral hood on infants, children, and many women would necessarily lead to the cutting and damaging of the clitoral shaft and the clitoris itself, as well as the labia. Of course, there is also the risk of infection and excessive bleeding and the certainty of trauma.

If such "procedures" were ever permitted, there would be no ability actually to review whether the microscopic area of the clitoral hood of an infant or small girl were not actually scarred, setting aside the lifetime of associated psychological oppression carried with the ritual. Scar tissue from "nicking," particularly on women prone to keloid scarring (as many women of color are) and difficult healing, can inhibit erogenous response and cause discomfort.

8
Fighting for Victory against Islamism

A blueprint for how the West can counter Islamist tyranny.

National Review

December 16, 2015 9:00 AM

How much more slaughter of innocents in the name of Islam do we need to endure before the free nations of the world wake up and admit that we are at war with the ideology of Islamism? We are in a global struggle of a magnitude we have not seen since the end of the Cold War — and this time we are fighting an enemy whose natural constituency includes almost one-fourth of the world's population.

The steady drumbeat of Islamist violence around the world has now reached a climax with the horrific atrocities in Paris and San Bernardino. No longer can pseudo-experts, apologists, and the media hide behind excuses, platitudes, and clichés. Enough is enough.

America's military, intelligence, and security agencies

will continue to operate a sophisticated and expensive whack-a-mole program as long as they look only at the final stages of radicalization. Before an individual takes a turn toward violence and dons the military vest and weaponry of an Islamist soldier, he spends years wearing the jersey of the Islamist team. As long as we focus only on the weaponized Islamist, and not all Islamists, we are in a state of unmitigated surrender. Our current approach surrenders the Western values of liberty embodied in our constitutional republic to the strangulation of political Islam and the massive Islamist movements across the planet.

Imagine if the Cold War had been fought by monitoring and countering only acts of Soviet-inspired violence rather than their enormous ideological domestic and global precursors? The West would have lost the war.

The same is true in the struggle against Islamism, also known as theocratic or political Islam. The West desperately needs a broad-based anti-Islamist strategy to combat the global reach of this deadly ideology that threatens freedom and liberty everywhere. The "Evil Empire" of today is the Organization of Islamic Cooperation (OIC), comprising 56 Muslim-majority nations that are the cauldrons of political Islam.

Taking the side of reform-minded Muslims who champion liberty and eschew Islamism must be the centerpiece of the strategy. American Muslims, living in this unparalleled laboratory of freedom, have a unique moral obligation to lead the way. For too long we have allowed the grievance narratives of Islamist groups to dominate, deflect responsibility, and radicalize. As American Muslims, we need to own the problem and address the root causes of Islamist radicalization.

For too long we have allowed the grievance narratives of Islamist groups to dominate, deflect responsibility, and radicalize.

To that end, freedom-loving Muslims need their own declaration of principles. Such a Muslim declaration can not only chart a course for reform but also become the centerpiece of thinking on almost every other policy question on which Muslim leaders, mosques, and organizations are working for the protection of universal human rights, versus those antagonists or apologists who are working against us.

Earlier this month our American Islamic Forum for Democracy held a foundational Summit of Western Muslim Reformists against the Islamic State and Islamism, held on December 2–4. This summit was a decade in the making, as our diverse anti-Islamist Muslim coalition from the U.S., Canada, and Europe slowly came together. But fate would have it that our planned summit convened only weeks after the second horrific ISIS-inspired attacks in Paris and the same day as the San Bernardino attack.

We concluded the summit proclaiming the co-founding of the Muslim Reform Movement and presenting to the world our Declaration, in which for the first time we put the Islamist movement and its insurgent ideas on the defensive. Our declaration lays down an ideological firewall inside the House of Islam between our Movement and the Islamists. Watch the press conference and get to know these courageous leaders, whom I'm proud to call friends and colleagues: Tahir Gora, Tawfik Hamid, Usama Hasan, Arif Humayun, Farahnaz Ispahani, Naser Khader, Hasan Mahmud, Courtney Lonergan, Asra Nomani, Raheel Raza, Sohail Raza, and Salma Siddiqui. Other Muslims will choose sides, and we pray that thought leaders and policy-makers choose the side of religious liberty in a war of ideas known all too well by our Founding Fathers.

The Muslim Reform Movement is united in our common opposition to theocracy and tyranny. Many more Muslims who dissent from Islamism have already come forward to join us in just the past week, gathering strength from our resolve and from the clarity of the platform we are creating.

We are harboring no illusions. But before the hard work of theological reform even begins to come together, we needed to first chart a destination and set our moral compass. We cannot roll up our sleeves until we know who our allies really are. We claim no ownership of the mantle of reform, but we reject Islamists who falsely label their work within the Islamist movement as "reform." The old pseudo-reformers who simply repackage Islamism — like Tariq Ramadan and Yusuf Qaradawi — cannot breach our firewall. The Islamist clerics and leaders in the West have already done us a service by revealing themselves in their Letter to Baghdadi. Their bombastic defense of violent jihadism, caliphism, and Islamism stands in stark contrast to our simple declaration.

We have firmly made the distinction between false reformers who simply modernize the face of Islamism and anti-Islamists who want to bring the House of Islam into compatibility with universal human rights.

#share# The nine precepts of the declaration of our Muslim Reform Movement fall into three categories: "Peace: National Security and Counterterrorism Policy," "Human Rights," and "Secular Governance." We believe that Muslims who can embrace these precepts and Americans who can embrace those Muslims will be on the right side of history as we lead the global war against Islamist movements.

The full two-page declaration can be signed online by fellow Muslims and our supporting neighbors at Change. org. Help us grow at Facebook. The declaration is a full-throated defense of freedom, free speech, critical thinking, gender equality, minority rights, secular governance, democracy, and the separation of mosque and state. We also declare an unequivocal condemnation of all Islamic states, caliphism, violent jihad, institutionalized sharia, blasphemy laws, and apostasy laws. Three defining principles are worth noting here:

> *"We believe ideas do not have rights. Human beings do."*
> *"Our ummah — our community — is not just Muslims, but all humanity."*
> *"Muslims don't have an exclusive right to heaven."*

In the spirit of iconic reformers, we marched after our December 4 press conference and posted our declaration on the doors of the mosque that is part of the Saudi-government-affiliated Islamic Center of Washington on Massachusetts Avenue in D.C. Officials of the Center ripped it down, and we dialogued with them. We await their formal response.

We will go on and ask our communities to present these foundational, inviolable precepts of reform to every Muslim leader, organization, and mosque that we can in our respective nations. Any who sign on will be with us in reform and counter-radicalization. Any who do not are part of the radicalization problem and obstacles to reform.

We do not seek to criminalize nonviolent Islamism, but instead to shine a bright light upon their archaic, corrupt ideology. We will compile a database of the responses to our declaration, and hope it will become a centerpiece of conversation and policy-making in the West. No longer will we need guesswork and innuendo to determine if a particular Muslim is part of the global Islamist platform and programming.

American Muslim leaders must state clearly that the Islamist ideology needs to be defeated, not merely contained.

There are many antecedents for our declaration, starting with Martin Luther's 95 Theses and going on to the Declaration of Independence, the U.S. Constitution, the Bill of Rights, the Universal Declaration of Human Rights, and the Sharon Statement, drafted by M. Stanton Evans under the aegis of William F. Buckley Jr. in 1960. Each defined a movement. The Sharon Statement, reflecting the ideological struggle of the time, said that "Communism must be defeated, not merely contained."

American Muslim leaders must state clearly that the Islamist ideology needs to be defeated, not merely contained. For Buckley and his colleagues, the enemy was the tyranny of Soviet Communism. Today, the enemy is the global threat of Islamism.

As a Midwestern-born American Muslim, the child of Syrian political refugees fleeing the tyranny of Ba'athism,

I proudly donned the uniform of the U.S. Navy for eleven years. I joined the Navy to be a part of the military forces of the nation that gave my family freedom and represented the most moral force for good under God on the planet.

#related# Militant Islamists are bred, contrarily, in a theo-political culture where their soul, identity, and self worth are inexorably wedded to Islamo-patriotism — the assertion of the supremacy of the Islamic state. They act for the tribe, and reject even the implication that individual rights "under God" might be possible for all through a secular government. Understanding this consciousness is crucial. Freedom-loving Muslims must fight for an Islam that rejects the Islamists as the real blasphemers and enemy of mankind.

The Declaration of the Muslim Reform Movement puts the Islamists on the defensive and gives birth to a counter-Islamist offensive based in the ideas of religious liberty and universal human rights. We are ready ideological warriors for the nation. The security of the United States, Israel, and the West hangs in the balance.

9
Can a Western Islam Emerge?
Radical Islam Anthology

October 2018

"New opinions are always suspected, and usually opposed, without any other reason but because they are not already common." – John Locke

In December 2017, the first Radical Islam Conference hosted by HJS led to the foundational establishment of a 'trans-Atlantic network' of counter-terrorism, counter-*jihadism* experts. This is vitally important to the security of Western civilisation. As an American Muslim, I have dedicated my life to educating everyone I can, and doing everything that I can, to expose and address the root causes of Islamism (aka Political Islam). once we have a public consensus that Islamism is the problem, it will become natural to promote the ideas of liberty and universal human rights within Muslim communities as the solution.

It is essential that diverse anti- and counter-jihadists work together in what we are doing in the West to minimise redundancy and amplify progress. With the ever-changing map of leadership across government, media, academia, and faith communities, the few thought leaders that understand the threat of Salafi-Jihadism need to amplify our voices to continuously educate Western leadership.

The role of reform-minded Muslim voices against Islamist leadership cannot be overemphasized. Muslims courageous enough and honest enough to face the dominant influence of Islamists inside and outside Muslim communities will need the strong shoulders of long established thought leaders and government influencers to stand on, since we are the only ones who can break through the false grievance narratives of Islamist groups.

Islamists have made a cottage industry out of promulgating a false premise of bigotry (aka Islamophobia – a word we should all reject) against anyone who is anti-Islamist. The premise of our work at the American Islamic Forum for Democracy is that in fact being anti-Islamist and pro-liberty is actually pro-Muslim and in support of a modernised, 21st century Islam. There would be nothing more pro-Muslim than helping peaceful Muslims shed the yolk of medieval interpretations of *shariah* and the inviolability of the Islamic jihadist state.

Importance of Identity

At the centre of our work is the synergy of personal identity and national identity. This synergy, or its countervailing conflict, for many Muslims is at the core of this work on reform and modernisation. My own personal history as a US naval officer and an avowed patriot is no aberration or mutation of Western Muslims, as some would say. In fact, I believe that this is the far more common narrative of a silent majority of Muslims in the West, who have abrogated the leadership of our communities to the Islamist theocrats. I was raised by patriotic American Muslim parents who were also strong adherents of their interpretation of the faith of Islam, and I know that there are a lot of Muslims out there who share my background and faithful underpinnings of my patriotism.

As a result of this passion for my nation, I joined the US navy on a medical school scholarship, and served 11 years as a medical officer, feeling from the outset that the only country I would ever die for is the United States of America. I also contrarily, if not similarly, believed that I never wanted to dream for, let alone work for, and especially die for *'Jihad'* or for *'Islam'*, as that for me was simply a personal concept related to my relationship with god. god never needed me to die for him. My grandparents and parents taught me that while god watches all that I do and I will be judged on my behaviour and integrity, I never needed to prove my faith though a single action and especially with the collective *ummah*.

I also understood that Islamist global movements tapped into this false premise that Muslims must be loyal to the global *"ummah"* and its *jihad*. So I actively rejected it. I also knew that Muslim leaders needed to make this rejection a dominant idea in the West, and eventually, globally.

I further realised that with the oppressive domination of Islamist regimes and their *shariah* based legal systems across Muslim majority nations (aka organisation of Islamic Cooperation, OIC), we have a unique responsibility in the West to use the laboratory of freedom to defeat Islamists.

All of this is unbelievably important to the security mission of our transatlantic network against Islamist terror. The only real way to counter Islamist radicalisation is to face the central power of familial, tribal, local, national, and global jihadist movements (like the Muslim Brotherhood). our identity as free Americans is the only way to inoculate faithful Muslims in their belief in god and nation, and against Islamist supremacism. I know that I am not unique. There are many Muslims, if not a majority, who are not primarily or even secondarily influenced by an *imam* or by a local community which influences or dictates their collective interpretation of faith. For many, even if they have some exposure to clerics and Islamist collectivists, they do not buy into the negation of self and negation of national identity involved in global jihadism for the *ummah*.

While I am of *Sunni* extraction, this conversation can be superimposed upon any Islamists within communities whether of *Shia*, *Sunni*, or other heterodox extractions. The ideology of political Islam and its attendant identity movements that seek to impose an Islamic state identity along with its *shariah* laws upon communities transcends sectarian divides. The sectarian divides may balkanise Islamists and their non-Islamist counterparts, but the reforms long overdue against Islamic state identity movements apply across essentially every sect of Islam.

How Will a Western Islam Emerge?

There has been some obvious spontaneity to the emergence of Western characteristics within various practices of Islam in the West, but I would submit that this is *despite* the concerted efforts of the Islamic leadership (the Islamist establishment of Muslim Brotherhood legacy group and their petro-Islamist benefactors) to prevent that modernisation and liberalisation. However, that neo-modern and neo-Islamist evolution has been entirely uncoordinated and completely overshadowed by an extraordinarily dominant Islamist network in the West and the various forms of military dictatorships across Muslim majority nations of the OIC. In the West, that network includes the vast majority of mosques and organised Islamic institutions.

There is little doubt that modern liberal interpretations of Islam have begun to evolve, but without a coordinated effort to unite those liberal movements (classically liberal) they will likely never have the influence and bandwidth to take on, let alone defeat, the Islamists.

Our Muslim Reform Movement, a coalition of very diverse Muslim leaders who share an enmity for Islamist ideologies and identities and share a passion for secular liberty and freedom, embraced our deep political and national differences from the US, Canada, and Europe and established our coalition on 4 December 2015. The defining element of our Muslim Reform Movement is the two-page Declaration of Principles that we diligently agreed upon and set forth as a defining document of our movement and our coalition. We believe that declaration lays out the central ideological differences between an oppressive Islamist worldview and a worldview based in universal human rights and liberty.

Our declaration can, and should be, used as a firewall to delineate which Muslims are on the side of a Westernised interpretation of Islam (our allies) and which are Islamist or Salafi-Jihadist (our enemies). The emergence of a Western Islam will be based on this legacy.

The bottom line for Muslims open to reform is that they believe, fundamentally, that there should be no intermediaries between a Muslim and god. There should be no intermediaries between a Muslim's independent interpretation of their faith and god. When we talk about the emergence of a Western Islam, this is important with regards to legacy. I believe that any Muslim that will embrace and be part of leading this reform movement is going to be from those that deeply care about the Islam that our kids and our kids' kids will have. only the Muslim leaders courageous enough to take on Islamist thinkers and use Western ideas as a starting point against the root of the cancer that is Islamism will be helpful.

So the Question Is How Do We Get There? What Is the Optimal, Most Strategic Western Response?

Using a football analogy, I want to give you the definition that I feel is in the end zone (the goal post), at the other end of the field we are headed across in this battle. yes, whilst we might be at the one-yard line on the other end of the field, what can the goal post represent?

Western Islam in my eyes is a modern, free Islam, rooted in universal human rights, that gives Muslims the freedom to embrace national identities in their primary loyalty of citizenship rooted first and foremost in reason, and liberty, rather than theocracy and *shariah* state. I believe that is where we are headed, or where we think will ultimately be a universal type of Islam that can feel comfortable in any secular liberal democracy. So how do we get there?

The First Question Is Who Is the 'We'?

I think it is important that non-Muslims realise that this is not just our problem to be solved within the House of Islam. If we Muslims get this wrong, a quarter of the world's population will continue to be ruined by various forms of theocracy and repression. Eventually, in some form or another, the West will continue to be collateral damage to those theocracies and their neo-caliphate. Make no mistake. The *caliphate* exists today, and it is called the oIC. It is a 'neo-caliphate', and if left to their own devices, many of those Islamist nations may end up destroying each other across sectarian divides like that between Saudi Arabia and Iran. But ultimately, the entire oIC unites in a Machiavellian way fomenting the idea of a common non-Muslim enemy. Islamists in their *caliphate* divide the world into the *Dar-al-Islam* and *Dar-al-Harb*. Those of us living outside Muslim majority countries are considered to be living in the 'land of war'. The only evolution out of this paralysing, fossilised concept of Islamic and non-Islamic lands of peace and war is for Muslims to redefine *"ummah"*, from only Muslims, to include all of humanity. That is the premise of our Muslim Reform Movement: we are citizens of our secular nations and we reject the attachment of our Islamic faith identity to our national identities.

Prisoners of conscience from many of these nations need to become household names. Saudi prisoner of conscience, Raif Badawi, needs to become a household name. We need a whole of government strategy, from Department of State (DoS) to Department of Defence (DoD) to the White House which takes the information war against Islamism on the offense. We need to restart the same process as the Cold War but this time against Islamism rather than communism.

Look at our Declaration of the Muslim Reform Movement. Those principles can be used on the granular level for vetting individuals as to whether or not they adhere to Islamism and it can also be applied to groups and even nation states. For example, should Turkey be part of NATO? Erdogan would never agree to many of the premises of our Declaration. So the answer is no.

In a discussion on the emergence and viability of a Western Islam, I prefer to think of an Islam that embraces the Universal Declaration of Human Rights. In my opinion, the West does not have a monopoly on universal liberty or universal human rights. All humanity essentially is created with an innate desire to be free.

The question for 'we' Muslim reformers is, what is the division in the world today? The easiest division to look at leading Muslims is to boil it down to either 'revivalists or reformers'. *Revivalists* like the *Salafis* look backwards and want to bring back Islam at the time of the 7th century when it was first revealed, whatever their interpretation of it as they see through the *hadith*. Contrarily, *reformers*, for the most part, look forward and only hold on to that tradition which is not in conflict with the moral substance of a nation under god, and based in liberty for all. So if Salafis (*salaf* being friends of the Prophet) look backward, are all Islamists Salafists and are all Salafists Islamists? The best differentiation I have heard between Salafis and Islamists is that the Salafis use politics for religious control (as we see in Saudi Arabia) while the Islamists use religion for political control (as we see with the Muslim Brotherhood). The bottom line is that they are all drinking from the same trough and the same intoxicant – Islamism and its Islamic *shariah* state. The Islamists may pretend to look forward and have a 'neo-Salafi' way of modernising the old Islamic state, but theirs is still an Islamist state under *shariah* no matter how they try to mollify it or modernise it in Islamism 2.0, 3.0, or 4.0. The end of the Islamic state concept will be the demise of both Islamism and Salafism.

In the End It Is All About Driving Legacy

The question for 'reformers' as opposed to 'revivalists' is simple. The way we came up with our declaration is by asking ourselves, if the Prophet Mohammed were alive today, what would be the type of society, the type of state he would want to see as the ideal society? our vision draws from the many enlightenment principles that John Locke, Thomas Jefferson, and James Madison instilled into Western democracies through governments like the US, that have an Establishment Clause which protects against theocracy. Many tell us we need someone like a Martin Luther King in Islam. But, the evolution of a new school of thought in Islamic law, *shariah*, will take generations. We first need leaders and societies which allow that work to be done. We first need a John Locke. We need thought leaders who are able, within an Islamic identity, to separate religion from politics. Upon those foundations of citizenship within a liberal democratic identity, a future unravelling of Islamist *shariah* is bound to happen.

In this generation, we do have time to create networks that can lift up secular liberals that allow us to re-brand western universal principles as also Muslim principles. That is exactly what we do in some of our projects. When I talk to Muslim parents, I ask them to tell me the top 10 ideas that they think characterise Muslim culture. They talk about honesty, integrity, sanctity of family, and all these principles. I say if you can teach your kids these exact same things without using the brand of *Islam* or *sh*ariah, you can do it simply based on values and moral principles which are also the basis of Judeo-Christian principles. Almost universally, every one of them says I would rather have my son or daughter embrace an honest Christian or a Jewish community than a traditional externally appearing religious, praying, covered Muslim that lies and is deceitful.

So in essence, you can say the key to a Western Islam is rooted in a societal identity based in morality, liberty, and equality, rather than what theocrats impose in an Islamist system.

The influence of state media from Saudi Arabia or Qatar's *Al Jazeera* or Iran's *PressTV* and all the Islamist social media bandwidths directly influence and dominate Muslim opinions in the US and in Europe. The only way to counter these tyrannical theocratic influencers is here in our laboratory of freedom. This anti-Islamist work cannot happen yet in Egypt or necessarily in Iraq, and definitely not in Syria, Iran, or Saudi. The oIC governments just do not allow the critical thinking necessary, and they certainly would not allow a non-Islamic state identity to evolve.

Eventually, just like the evolution of Americanism, Egyptians, Tunisians and others will need to determine what exactly their uniting 'Egyptianism' or 'Tunisianism' is, and if it will be based in universal principles or draconian Islamist ones. That is what we need to operationalise throughout the world, domestically and globally, and is the basis of our Muslim Reform Movement. The West can facilitate this by clearly defining which Muslims and their movements are allies sharing their beliefs in universal rights. For example, those Muslim allies must reject all violent *jihad*, reject the Islamic State, reject the existence of a *caliphate*, believe in equality between men and women, believe in the inviolability of free speech, and the religious freedom of all, including Muslims, to leave their faith.

We Must Go on the Offence

For too long, we have been on the defence. The Islamists are far ahead of us in their global strategy because they live on the offence and have pushed the West for too long into the defence. *Dawah* is their missionary work, spreading and educating Islamism abroad and moving forward their political movement (offence). Are we in the West contrarily doing a metaphorical *dawah* for liberty (offence)? For secular liberal democracy? no, I don't think that's part of our forward strategy and I used *dawah* as a metaphor obviously, but we desperately need to start an offence where we put those Islamists and Salafists on the defence. We need to go far beyond the current infinite whack-a-mole programme which just deals with terrorism, one end-point of the threat. They will keep coming back unless we confront Islamists. If we have an offence, we can then begin to chip away at their theocratic ideas with ideas of liberty and build allies in places as messy as Syria, Iran, and Saudi Arabia, but in the UK and in the US. That mission will ultimately inoculate Muslims against radicalisation.

Culture shifts what we focus on. We need to use this to our advantage to defeat the Islamist establishment. We have been completely out of the game of the cultural wars that the Islamists have been fighting, and it is long overdue that we have a platform and a voice in those battles. That is where the front line is.

Last, what do we do with passages of the Quran that have interpretations that are not compatible with modern society? We can either ignore them and cast them aside or modernise their interpretations. In fact, we likely need to do both. In order to have legitimacy within the vast majority of the Muslim faithful, the authenticity of the Arabic scripture of the Quran is inviolable. However, the narrative can be reformed about what time and place the passage applies to, or reading them beyond a literalism and simply applying an overriding principle or metaphor in light of modern day morality and identities (*ijtihad*).

If you were to stage this evolution of reform of a

Western Islam, the first stage is creating the movement of those who are sick and tired of the clerics of the Islamic establishment. Then the second stage is developing a Muslim identity outside the currently Islamist-dominated mosques. We have to help create, however small they may be, organisations and institutions that are Islamic yet rooted in Western principles.

Third, the West needs to take sides (in a whole-of-society approach) and define who our allies are, and realise this is a bi-partisan affair; it is not just, simply "the Muslim issue" as a wedge issue. The denial that the root cause of radicalisation and the enemy of freedom is Islamism must stop.

10
An Epilogue From
A Battle for the Soul of Islam: An American Patriot's Fight to Save his Faith

A Letter to My Children

Dear Zachariah, Zaina, and Zaid,

On occasion you have asked me, What is this book you're writing? What kind of story is it? An adventure? Is there a bad guy? Who wins?

All very good questions, of course. In its way, it is an adventure, but probably not one you will want to read until you get a bit older, since you are barely ten, eight, and four. With that in mind, I'm writing you this letter in a way that will also make more sense to you when you are older because some of the things it addresses are very much from the world of grown-ups. But what kind of adventure is the book, you may ask, and I will answer: the one of our country and our faith. You ask if there is a bad guy, and I tell you there are, in fact, many bad guys and bad women, and many good guys and good women.

Just over a year ago, members of our U.S. Navy SEAL Team Six killed a very bad man named Osama Bin Laden. You, Zachariah, have had questions about that. Who was this man? Was he bad? Why did they call him a Muslim? It would have been so much easier for me to just tell you, "He's not a Muslim." But that is between him and God. What I do know and have explained to you is that he was very bad, that he sent men to kill our fellow Americans on September 11, 2001, a few months before you were born, and unfortunately, they were very successful in their mission.

Thousands of innocent Americans died: fathers, mothers, even children of all faiths and national origins. It was a terrible day for this country and for the world. How do I explain why a man would send other men to do such a terrible thing? I can't, really, other than to say there is a thing called "evil" in the world. It is very real. All of us every day are confronted by evil. In the Qur'an God refers to *shaitan,* or the devil, as the source, a metaphor, of all evil putting those ideas into our head. It is all basically a sign of free will. We cannot understand good if we have never known evil. We cannot understand health if we have never known sickness. We all have to decide what is wrong and what is right. If we intentionally choose what is wrong,

God sees and knows all.

Everyone is taught right and wrong, but people have many different ideas about what makes something right and what makes it wrong. There is, however, a simple way for you to know if you are doing the right or the wrong thing. If what you do does more harm than good, then you can know you're doing the wrong thing, and if it helps people, then it is the right thing. If three thousand hungry people receive food, it is something good. If three thousand innocent people are killed, there is no good in that, only evil.

When Bin Laden was killed, millions of people around our country celebrated. That may strike you as strange. You have asked me, isn't it wrong to kill? Yes, of course, killing is a terrible thing, but in the case of Bin Laden his death may end up saving thousands of lives, because Bin Laden lived to kill. Why? Because he was evil. Our nation was at war since he had declared war on us.

He claimed to kill others for the sake of Islam, and that he had God's blessing to do so. But the fact that people say that they do things in the name of God does not automatically make them good people. We judge others' goodness, or the lack of it, by their actions. Bin Laden prayed. He read the Qur'an, but it was almost as though he read a different book from the one you and I read and the scripture you and I recite when we do our daily prayers.

He thought the Qur'an, which was dictated in our Arabic language to the Prophet Muhammad by God through the Angel Gabriel, gave him the words with which he could explain how he could kill innocent men, women, and children. But tell me, what kind of God would tell others to kill the innocent? Bin Laden may have thought he was a holy man, but his actions showed him to be pure evil.

Live your life so that others will look at you and say, there goes a good man or woman. There goes someone who is kind, who does not look down on others, who helps the unfortunate of this world and knows that God sees all we do and all we think. Live your life to love others, whatever faith they may have, whether they are Christians, Jews, Muslims, Bahai, Buddhists, Hindus, or if they have no religion at all, but love them, treat them with respect and charity, no matter how different they may seem from you, for God has made the world with many different people, and our challenge on any given day is to love and love still more. Our challenge is not based on our success in this world, but only that God knows that for any given day, you tried your best to meet all of our challenges with the gifts we are each blessed with having.

You will know if you tried your best. But only God will know if and when you do it from humility or from arrogance. Bin Laden believed that his faith was better than other people's, even other Muslims, that only he had the answers, and others did not have the right to disagree with him, that only he knew what was right for the world. Would you like someone like that for your friend? Probably not. Is that what God teaches us to be? Of course not. Stand up for what you believe to be right, but if what you are calling right is hurting many other people, it must be wrong.

In a way, that is what my book is all about: trying to do the right thing by our faith and our country, and in the process trying to help as many people as possible. Bin Laden was the worst example of what happens when Muslims depart from the part of our faith that is beautiful and personal and make it into a global political movement that it is not meant to be. Bin Laden was not just one man, and he was not crazy. He was a natural product of dangerous ideas. I know you are proud of my work as a doctor.

Trust me. He was a sign, a symptom of a much deeper disease—Islamism. Know it. Understand it. Defeat it.

I want you to embrace your faith, to know that God is always with you, and at the same time I want you to love your country, to know that it is very special, like no other in the world, and that it gives you great freedoms just as God has given you many blessings.

Please, never let your faith be something that you use to

hurt other people, but rather let it be a bridge, something with which you build understanding and friendships and love. Learn your religion and be disciplined in its scholarship, but feel free to set your own path and rely on your own conscience once you've done all your reading and asking. Questioning leaders, imams, and scholars is central to Islam and being human. As much as I and your mother will always pray for you, in the end you will be judged by God alone without anyone at your side, even your parents. Show everyone you meet love, but some may need tough love. Don't let the pressure of the tribe sway you from what is right. If you love God, rely on Him, stay humble, and remain true to your values, all will work out. Don't allow anyone or any government to get between you and God. Never let anyone into that space.

As to your country, please always be willing to give something back. I joined the Navy when I was younger because I wanted to give something back. I became a physician because I wanted to give something back. I started the American Islamic Forum for Democracy some years ago because I wanted to give something back, and because after 9/11 I thought it was important that American Muslims stand in defense of both their country and their faith and make it clear to the world that we as Muslims took responsibility for repairing our own house. It is great to live in a free country, and one in which there are many wonderful things to enjoy, but it is also important to stand up for something, and to fight against evil. Our parents, your grandparents, came to America not to bring Islam here, but rather to appreciate freedom and bring the values of liberty into our faith.

I hope you can understand, even at your young ages, that both faith and freedom call us to action. They are both gifts, but they must not be taken for granted. They must be cherished and defended, just as you would with those you love. You take care of them, stand up for them when you have to, and show your loyalty and love through your actions. Your grandparents and your great grandparents knew what it was like to live without freedom, but fortunately, they never knew what it was like to live without faith.

They believed that God would help them as they struggled to form a new life in America, and He did. Perhaps your motherland of Syria will begin to know and taste real freedom soon? Getting rid of an evil tyrant like Assad is only the first major obstacle. My hope for you is that your faith will always provide you with the inner strength to meet any challenge and that our country will always offer you the freedom you need to make your dreams come true. Know that already you are living lives that your grandparents and great-grandparents only dreamed of, and this is because of their brave actions, and all the actions of many men and women through the years, who make it their job to keep us safe and free. Some are soldiers, others police officers, or those who promote civil rights for all—the list could go on and on—but they all have one thing in common: They believe in the freedoms on which this country was founded, including freedom of religion. Here in the United States, we are more free to worship the way we choose as Muslims than we would be anywhere else on earth. Yet, we could lose all of our freedoms tomorrow, and we would still be Muslims and still be close to God. It would be all we'd have. But it would make it difficult for us to be human the way we are now, and have the opportunity to live, create, love, and enjoy each other. Our great nation and its great laws guarantee us our identity, our opportunity to live. Our faith can never be taken away and it is not for government to oversee, only to give us the freedom to practice it. At your young ages, it may be hard to take all that in, but through the years I hope and pray that you will make it your mission in whatever way you choose to give back to the country that has given us so much and to hold close the faith that has seen us through so many trials. In order to do so, you must carry the mantle against political Islam and for a spiritual, free Islam.

I have never had a conflict between my faith of Islam and my nation. I pray that I am able to live you that same gift that my parents gave me. Being a patriotic American, I worry deeply that most of the books on the shelves about Islam and being Muslim, whether written by Muslims or non-Muslims, could drive you away from that synergy and these ideas. I pray that you devote at least part of your own lives to helping Muslims in America and across the world advocate for liberty, and to seeing that my dream that political Islam wither on the vine of history and be replaced by an academic tradition of Islam that unequivocally separates mosque and state comes true. I hope and pray we can do our hajj to Mecca one day before our time on this earth is done. One of the ways that you may know that Islam has been liberated from the shackles of Islamism is when the world can see that the nation that houses the Grand Mosque of Mecca is free and represents an Islam that embraces universal human rights and liberty. It saddens me so that the Kaaba, which is one of the central unifying spiritual symbols of our faith and history, the direction to which we all pray, is protected by a nation that violates most of the sacred humanitarian principles of life and our Islam. Instead they produce and toxically export Osama Bin Laden, Al Qaeda, Islamism, Salafism, Wahhabism and impose on their people one of the most oppressive xenophobic regimes in the world. The birthplace of Islam neither belongs to the House of Saud nor any single Muslim.

It belongs to all Muslims, to God. No nation and its

people should ever belong to a tribe. Countries and citizens should be free with unalienable rights and never owned by a family. When the citizens of Saudi Arabia are free and their petrodollars are used to spread freedom rather than Islamism, hate, and fascism, then our humanitarian dreams of liberty for all will finally begin to be realized.

Know that your mom and I and your grandparents are always with you in spirit in the depths of your heart, praying for your strength, clarity, and success. Success is neither measured in achievements nor material wealth but in your own sense of moral clarity and integrity. Always first remember God, and know that it is nations built upon values like those of our United States that give us the liberty and the opportunity to know Him and be Muslim or be any faith, equal before the law. I hope my story, my ideas, let you understand *why*. Your own stories will certainly be different. Chart your own course. The places you take your opportunities will be different. But I hope your morals, your values, and the context in which you place God, our nation, our law, and Islam are the same if not better. It is your responsibility to take our experiences, our ideas, and build your own upon them, and to leave this world a better place for your children than the one we left to you. There should never be a conflict in your heart or your mind between loving your country, the freest nation in the world, and loving your faith of Islam.

Your mother and I love you all more than we could ever put into words,and hope you can understand that more than anything else, my work and this book are for you.

www.ingramcontent.com/pod-product-compliance
Lightning Source LLC
Chambersburg PA
CBHW032056150426
43194CB00006B/552